The Art of Video Editing

Adobe Premiere Pro

By: Rahul Kumar

This book is dedicated to my parents

This book is dedicated to my parents, **Mr. Vijay Kumar Gupta and Mrs. Dewanti Devi**, and my big brothers, **Big B** Dipu Gupta and Vikash Gupta. Thank you for always inspiring me and standing by me in all situations.

A special thanks to my sister Sapna for her unwavering support and encouragement in my studies and writing endeavours.

To my Bhabhi Rohini and Raushni, thank you for your support and Love.

To my entire Gupta family, especially my mother, who is my backbone and heart, thank you.

This book is dedicated to the cherished memory of my **grandparents, Late Kanhaiya Prasad Sah and Late Bindwashni Devi**. Their wisdom, love, and enduring legacy continue to inspire me every day. May this work honor their memory and reflect the values they instilled in me.

Lastly, I want to acknowledge myself for writing this book. This book embodies my whole heart and my extensive experience in video editing.

The Art of Video Editing: Adobe Premiere Pro

1st Edition

Author: **Rahul Kumar**

Grammar and Spelling: **Dipu Gupta**

Rewrite: **Shashank**

Design**: Rahul Kumar (Studio Manager, Amity University)
Cover Design & Mock Up: Crazy Harsh Raj**

Book Layout: **Mr. Kumar Vishal (Academic Co-ordinator, Amity University)**

Publishing Year: 2024

Special Thanks: Ribha Kumari, Ekta Chauhan, Chirag Manocha, Mayanak Tiwari, Sai Krishna, Samuel Jitesh Raj, Akash Mithu, Prabhash Singh, Rahul Yadav, Ravi, Raunak Yadav, Ratan Yadav ,Chandan

---

Special Note:

This book is for educational purposes only. This book is a result of experiences in relevant field. The author has only shared their experience and do not claim to be the 100% accurate of the information. Please read more relevant material to get confirmation of information. In case if you find error kindly inform us via email so that we can improve it in another editions.

Images are from a Live Video project, and some images representing live editing techniques are taken from Adobe Premiere Pro.

Any suggestions or feedback? Please connect with the author at: **contact2rahulkr@gmail.com**

About Book

There are many people who want to build their career in the field of editing, and not just a career but also want to build an empire in the field of editing by doing something innovative. The field of editing is distinct from all other fields and is vast, requiring a large amount of time to comprehend and fully understand it.

However, to succeed in this domain, one must constantly acquire knowledge and put effort in the field of editing. By producing creative and noteworthy work, one can establish a presence in the global arena.

In order to make a good film, collaboration of the entire team is needed. In the same way, this book will help you in understanding and learning better about editing.

This comprehensive guide to Adobe Premiere Pro is designed for students and video production professionals who aspire to build successful careers in video production and video editing. Whether you are a beginner looking to learn the basics or a seasoned professional seeking to enhance your skills, this book provides the tools and insights needed to excel in the dynamic world of video editing.

Purpose of this Book

This book is designed to be a comprehensive guide for both beginners and seasoned professionals in the realm of video editing.

It will delve into the fundamentals of the craft, explore advanced techniques, discuss emerging trends and technologies, and provide practical insights into building a successful career in video editing. Whether you're a filmmaker seeking to refine your storytelling skills or an aspiring editor looking to enter the world of visual storytelling, this book aims to be your companion on the exciting journey of video editing.

Let's embark on this exploration of the art and craft that brings moving images to life on the screen.

The purpose of this book is to educate students and aspiring editors on the crucial role of video editing in everyday life. It aims to inspire readers to think critically about the art of editing and understand its significance. The book introduces Adobe Premiere Pro, a leading software in video editing, providing fundamental knowledge for beginners. It explores the necessity of learning video editing, highlighting its major applications across various sectors.

Additionally, it delves into the latest trends and technologies in the field, ensuring readers are well-equipped with contemporary skills and insights.

Acknowledgements

Writing a comprehensive guide on the art of video editing wouldn't have been possible without the support, encouragement, and expertise of numerous individuals and organizations

I would like to express my deepest appreciation to **Dr. Vivekanand Pandey, Honourable Vice Chancellor of Amity University Patna**, Sir guidance and leadership have been instrumental in the completion of this book. Sir steadfast support has been instrumental in shaping the content and direction of this publication.

Sincere thanks to **Professor Prof. Sweta Priya, Head of the Amity School of Communication at Amity University Patna**, for her invaluable guidance and feedback on this book. Her profound insights into communication and media studies have greatly enriched our work, ensuring its relevance and impact within the academic community.

I am also deeply grateful to **Professor Soummay Ghosh and Prof. Badshah Alam** for their exceptional mentoring and guidance. Their insights and expertise have profoundly enriched this work.

I convey sincere thanks to the professors at the Amity School of Communication (ASCO), especially to **Professor Rahul Ahuja, Professor Naveen Kumar, Professor Junny Kumari, Professor Shatabdi Chakraborty** and **Mr. Vishal Kumar** for creating an environment that fosters innovation in the workplace. Their suggestions and guidance have been crucial to getting a better result.

Grateful to Team ASCO.

Thank you all for making this endeavour possible

My family and friends for their endless encouragement, understanding, and patience during the long hours spent researching, writing, and editing this book.

Mr. Rahul Kumar is deeply inspired by **Prof. Sweta Priya**, **Prof. Soummay Ghosh, and Shatabdi Chakraborty** for their invaluable support and guidance in writing this book. He extends a special thanks and heartfelt gratitude to each of them for their encouragement and mentorship throughout this journey.

Specially I would like to **thank the readers of this book.**

With gratitude,

Rahul Kumar

About Author

Rahul Kumar is a passionate advocate for the power of visual storytelling and communication. With a background rooted in mass communication and a specialization in new media technology, Rahul brings a wealth of knowledge and experience to the world of video editing and content creation.

Currently serving as the **Studio Manager at Amity University Patna**, Rahul plays a pivotal role in the Department of **Amity School of Communication**. In this capacity, he oversees the production of multimedia content, manages studio resources.

Rahul's journey in the field of communication began with a bachelor's degree in mass communication from Patna College, where he honed his skills in journalism, broadcasting, and media production. Eager to stay ahead of the curve in the rapidly evolving landscape of digital media, he pursued a Post-Graduation in New Media Technology from Makhanlal Chaturvedi National University of Journalism and Communication.

Throughout his academic and professional career, Rahul has demonstrated a keen eye for detail, a flair for creativity, and a commitment to excellence. Whether crafting compelling narratives, experimenting with cutting-edge technologies, or mentoring the next generation of storytellers, Rahul is dedicated to pushing the boundaries of visual communication.

Beyond his professional endeavours, Rahul is an avid enthusiast of cinema, photography, poetry and digital art. He believes in the transformative power of media to inspire, educate, and bring about positive change in society.

About Chapter Writer:

Soummay Ghosh: Mr. Soummay Ghosh is an enthusiastic educator in journalism and mass communication. He is UGC-NET qualified and is currently serving as an assistant professor in the **Amity School of Communication at Amity University Patna**. His teaching methodology revolves around practical learning tools, ensuring comprehensive understanding among students. He incorporated real-world examples into the classroom instructions. He has done background music for the Nagpuri regional film "Dahleez." He has directed indie films like "Dil Haara" and "Laal Rang.". He is well known in academia and industry for his creativity and technology expertise.

Ribha Kumari: Ribha Kumari works at **AIIMS Patna** and holds a master's degree in social work from Patna Women's College. A passionate video production enthusiast, she excels in various types of video editing and is a dedicated tech enthusiast. As the author of the chapter on specialized video editing, Ribha offers valuable insights into different editing techniques and research. Her extensive knowledge and practical experience make her contribution an essential part of this book, providing readers with the skills and inspiration needed to excel in the field of video editing.

Akash Kumar: Akash Kumar, the author of the chapter on the history of video editing, brings a wealth of experience and creative influence on his work. Currently **employed at REC Limited**, he has made significant contributions to the growth of various projects, showcasing his expertise in video production and editing. Akash Kumar's career is marked by his dynamic roles, including collaborations with the Bihar government's Department of Information and Public Relations.

Shashank Parbat: Shashank Parbat completed his education up to the 12th grade in the Chapra district of Bihar before relocating to Patna, where he enrolled in the journalism programme at Amity School of Communication at Amity University Patna. This decision proved to be transformative, as he acquired a wealth of knowledge and developed a keen interest in editing., he made valuable contributions to various short films, such as Laal Rang, Saubhagyavati Bhava, Aakhri Muskaan, and Chamni. Shashank Parbat's journey in filmmaking also includes a notable role in the short film " Saubhagyavati Bhava versatility and dedication to the craft.

INTRODUCTION

Welcome to the exciting world of video editing!

In this comprehensive guide, we embark on a journey to uncover the secrets, techniques, and principles that define the art of video editing. Whether you're a budding filmmaker, a content creator, or simply curious about the magic behind the screen, this book is your ultimate companion on the path to mastering the craft.

Video editing is more than just a technical skill—it's a form of storytelling. Just as a painter uses brushes and colours to create a masterpiece, a video editor utilizes various tools and techniques to weave together visual narratives that captivate, inspire, and move audiences. From short films to commercials to social media content, effective editing can elevate ordinary footage into extraordinary experiences.

In this book, we'll start by laying the groundwork, exploring the definition and importance of video editing in today's digital landscape. We'll delve into real-world examples, showcasing how video editing transforms raw footage into compelling stories that resonate with viewers. Through relatable anecdotes and practical insights, we'll demystify the art of video editing, making it accessible to beginners and seasoned professionals alike.

But mastering video editing isn't just about learning technical skills—it's about cultivating creativity, intuition, and storytelling prowess. That's why we'll delve into the creative process, exploring techniques for crafting narrative flow, enhancing visual appeal, and evoking emotion through editing.

Whether you're editing a short film, a documentary, or a social media clip, you'll discover how to leverage the power of editing to engage, entertain, and inspire your audience.

Throughout this journey, we'll also trace the evolution of video editing technologies, from the days of linear editing systems to the era of cloud-based solutions. We'll examine the role of the video editor in the creative process, celebrating their contributions as storytellers, visual artists, and problem solvers.

So, are you ready to unlock your creativity, unleash your imagination, and embark on a journey into the heart of video editing?

Let's dive in and discover the artistry, innovation, and magic that await us in the world of video editing.

Together, we'll learn, create, and make our mark on the ever-evolving landscape of visual storytelling.

Dear Reader,

I have no doubt that you will read this book thoroughly well and understand every aspect of editing.

After reading and understanding all the chapters of the Book "The Art of Editing", you will learn and understand how a small amount of raw footage can be made into a theatre level film or an impactful video through Video editing.

So let us understand the chapters.

INDEX............

Chapter 1: History of Video Editing

Akash Kumar (Social Media Manager, REC Ltd)

The history of video editing is a fascinating journey that has evolved alongside advancements in technology and filmmaking. Here's a brief overview of the key milestones in the history of video editing:

Early Film Editing (Late 19th Century - Early 20th Century):

In the early days of filmmaking, editing was done manually by physically cutting and splicing together different film reels. This process was time-consuming and required great skill.

Linear Editing (1940s - 1970s):

Linear editing involved physically cutting and rearranging film strips in a sequential order. Editors used machines like the Moviola to splice together scenes, and the process was a linear progression from start to finish.

Introduction of Video Editing (1960s - 1970s):

With the advent of video technology, linear video editing systems emerged. Early systems like the Bosch Fernseh VCR and the Sony CV-2000 allowed editors to work with video footage. However, these systems were still linear in nature.

Non-Linear Editing (1980s - Present):

The introduction of non-linear editing (NLE) systems revolutionised the industry. With the advent of computers and digital technology, editors could now manipulate video files directly on a computer, making the editing process more flexible and efficient.

The first non-linear editing system was the CMX 600, introduced in 1971, but it wasn't until the 1980s that the technology became more widely available and affordable. Systems like Avid and Lightworks played a crucial role in popularising non-linear editing.

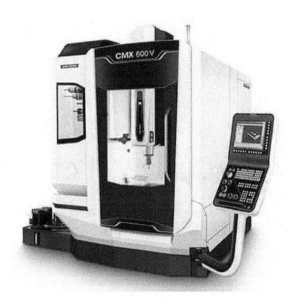

Non-linear editing system: CMX 600

Desktop Video Editing (1990s):

The 1990s saw the rise of desktop video editing with the introduction of software like Adobe Premiere and Apple Final Cut Pro. These applications brought professional-level editing capabilities to personal computers, making video editing more accessible to a broader audience.

Digital Video Revolution (2000s - Present):

The 2000s witnessed the widespread adoption of digital video formats, leading to higher quality and more accessible video production. High-definition (HD) and 4K resolutions became standard, and video editing software continued to evolve with features like real-time preview, advanced visual effects, and colour correction.

Cloud-Based Editing (2010s - Present):

With the rise of cloud computing, video editing has become more collaborative and accessible. Cloud-based editing platforms allow multiple users to work on the same project simultaneously, making it easier for teams to collaborate remotely.

Advancements in AI and Automation (2010s - Present):

Artificial intelligence (AI) and machine learning technologies have been integrated into video editing software, enabling features like automatic scene detection, content analysis, and even automated editing suggestions.

The history of video editing is a story of constant innovation driven by technological advancements, making it easier for creators to bring their visions to life on the screen.

Chapter 2: Introduction to Video Editing

Rahul Kumar (Studio Manager, Amity University Patna)

Video editing is a transformative process that takes raw footage and crafts it into a cohesive and engaging visual story. As technology has evolved, so too has the art and science of video editing, becoming an indispensable component in the filmmaking and content creation landscape.

Appreciate of Essence:

The talents of customize and swap round video footage/shots to create a seamless and compelling narrative. It involves angle, shots, movement and using editing techniques to communicate and convey the message to a mass no. of people.

Evolution of Video Editing:

The evolution of video editing began with manual, time-consuming methods that needed physically cutting splicing film reels. So, as digital technology created non-linear editing systems emerged allowing editors to work with greater freedom and efficiency.

The Role of the Video Editor:

A skilled video editor might be considered a digital canvas storyteller. They have acquired a great understanding of execution, a keen eye for detail, and the technical proficiency to navigate sophisticated editing software. Video editors are creative collaborators that offer a distinct viewpoint to the storytelling process.

The Role of a video editor is to develop raw footage to final output where the audience or final output make a large impact on the audience. Editing is not only to add and cut footage but also its work of keen eye for detail and the technical proficiency to navigate editing software. Video Editors works not only for making video ads and cutting unwanted footage but also to make the video catchier. Video editors should be storytellers. Just like a story's concept or moral, the editing of a video plays a crucial role in conveying the message, emotion, and impact.

Effective video editing can:

- Enhance the narrative

- Build tension or suspense

- Evoke emotions

- Create a sense of pace or rhythm

- Convey complex information in an engaging way

- Strengthen the overall impact

The impact of video is vast, and its role continues to evolve, shaping various aspects of our personal and professional lives.

Significance in Modern Media:

Video editing extends beyond traditional filmmaking and has become integral to various forms of modern media. From YouTube content creators to professional filmmakers, the ability to edit video is a powerful tool for communication and expression. Businesses leverage video editing to create marketing content, while educational institutions use it to enhance learning experiences.

2.1 Definition and Importance of Video Editing

Definition:

Video editing is the process of manipulating and rearranging video shots to create new work with the help of software. It involves selecting footage, trimming, arranging footage, and enhancing video footage to convey a specific message, tell a story, or evoke certain emotions.

Importance of Video Editing

Narrative: One of the finest and most powerful instruments for narrative is video editing. It allows creators to shape the narrative by controlling the pacing, sequence, and flow of scenes, ensuring that the story is engaging and effectively communicates the intended message.

Psychological Impact: The creators have the capacity to influence the audience's psychological reaction with accurate editing. The use of pacing, music, and visual elements can enhance the emotional impact of a video, making it more memorable and resonant.

Professionalism: Well-edited videos convey a sense of professionalism and attention to detail. Whether it's a short film, a promotional video, or an educational piece, polished editing reflects positively on the overall quality of the content.

Information Flow: The mechanism of information can be improved with video editing. Editors can ensure that the audience grasps and recalls information more effectively.

Expression and Creativity: Video editing is an art form that allows for creative expression. Editors can experiment with distinct approaches, effects, and aesthetics to provide their work a unique and innovative flair.

Adaptability: In the digital age, video content is created for various platforms and devices. Video editing enables creators to adapt their content for different formats, ensuring it remains engaging and impactful across a diverse range of viewing experiences.

Time Efficiency: The editing process has recently become far more rapid caused by nonlinear editing tools. Editors can make changes, experiment with different cuts and improve their work.

Collaboration: Collaborate with multiple editors and team members who can work together on the same project, which helps to enhance the overall creative process.

Marketability and Engagement: In the era of digitalisation, video content is one of the most engaging turbines. A perfect editing video helps to grab the attention of the viewers/public. A good editing video helps to boost shareability and marketability of the subject at hand.

In finalization, video editing is far more than just a technical technique; It is as vital element of visual narrative that mixes creativity and technical expertise.

2.2 Evolution of Video Editing Technologies

The evolution of video editing technologies is a captivating journey marked by significant advancements that have transformed the way we create and consume visual content. From the manual splicing of film reels to the sophisticated digital editing tools available today, the progression of video editing technologies has been instrumental in shaping the landscape of filmmaking and media production.

Manual Film Editing (Late 19th Century - Early 20th Century): Cutting and splicing film reels manually became the very first technique for video editing. Scenes were methodically pieced into place by editors by hand, a laborious endure that needed accuracy.

Linear Editing (1940s - 1970s): Linear editing systems were readily accessible between the 1940s and 1970s, allowing editors to arrange footage in a sequential order. splicing and playback have been submitted simpler by machines such as the Moviola, which simplified editing but limited creative freedom.

Introduction of Video Editing (1960s - 1970s): With the advent of video technology, linear video editing systems were introduced. Early systems, such as the Bosch Fernseh VCR and the Sony CV- 2000, allowed editors to work with video footage, bringing a new level of convenience compared to film.

Non-Linear Editing (1980s - Present): The debut of non-linear editing (NLE) innovation ignited a revolution. The CMX 600 in 1971 was an early example, but it wasn't until the 1980s that non-linear editing became more widely accessible. Digital editing was established viable through applications like Avid and Lightworks, which enabled editors to work using video files on a computer.

Desktop Video Editing (1990s): With the distribution of applications like Adobe Premiere and Apple Final Cut Pro, desktop video editing became more popular in the 1990s. These applications brought professional-level editing capabilities to personal computers, democratizing the editing process.

Digital Video Revolution (2000s - Present): The digital video revolution spanning the beginning of the 2000s to now. The widespread adoption of digital video formats became standard, offering higher quality and more accessible production. With features like real-time preview, complex visual effects, and color adjustment, video editing software continued to advance and high definition (HD) and 4k resolutions became the standard.

Cloud-Based Editing (2010s - Present): Cloud-based editing platforms were an outcome of cloud computing. These systems allow multiple users to collaborate on the same project remotely, streamlining the collaborative aspect of video editing.

Advancements in AI and Automation (2010s - Present): Artificial intelligence (AI) and machine learning technologies have been integrated into video editing software. The capacity to handle computerization into content analysis, scene identification and even editing recommendations has increased productivity and creativity.

Virtual and Augmented Reality Editing (2010s - Present):
The appearance of augmented reality (AR) and virtual reality (VR) has presented new opportunities and problems for the video editing industry. Editors now work with immersive environments, requiring specialized tools and techniques.

Technology for video editing has evolved as time passed, providing testimony of the industry's continuous attempts toward enhancing accessibility, creativity, and efficiency. From manual splicing to AI-driven automation, each era has contributed to the rich tapestry of video editing capabilities we have today. As technology continues to advance, the future promises even more exciting developments in the world of video editing.

2.3 Role of the Video Editor or Video Editor Work

Vital component in the filmmaking and content creation process is fulfilled by the video editor. Beyond the technical aspects of cutting and assembling footage, the video editor is a creative storyteller who shapes the narrative, controls the pacing, and influences the emotional impact of the final product. A variety of duties that go into creating a visually compelling story are included in the job description of a video editor.

Storytelling and Narrative Construction: Generating a riveting and convincing narrative is a video editor's major responsibility. This involves selecting the best shots, arranging scenes in a logical sequence, and ensuring that the story flows smoothly. To properly engage the audience, an editor needs to possess a profound comprehension of storytelling principles.

Velocity and Rhythm: Controlling the pacing of a video is a crucial aspect of the editor's role. Whether it's a calm meaningful moment or a furious action scene, the editor employs timing and rhythm to achieve the intended effect. This skill is essential for maintaining the audience's attention and guiding their emotional experience.

Selection of Shots and Footage: The video editor is responsible for choosing the most compelling and relevant shots from the raw footage. This demands a keen understanding of composition, an awareness of visual aesthetics, and the ability to identify the themes that enrich a story for an entire entity.

Collaboration with Directors and Producers: Collaboration is key in the filmmaking process. Video editors work closely with directors, producers, and other members of the creative team to understand the vision and goals of the project. Effective communication and collaboration contribute to a cohesive and successful product.

Sound Design and Audio Editing: Sound is an essential part of editing videos. Editors work on sound design, ensuring that the audio complements the visuals and enhances the overall viewing experience. This covers things like modifying dialogue, putting in sound effects and adding music.

Visual Effects and Post-Production Enhancements: Depending on the project, video editors may be involved in adding visual effects or enhancing certain aspects of the footage during post- production. This could involve colour correction, grading, and other visual enhancements to achieve the desired aesthetic.

Technical Proficiency: Beyond creativity, video editors need to be technically proficient in using editing software and understanding the latest technologies. This includes staying updated on industry trends, software updates, and emerging editing techniques.

Problem-Solving and Adaptability: During the postproduction phase, video editing frequently entails resolving difficulties. Editors need to be adaptable, creative problem-solvers who can find solutions to issues such as continuity errors, technical glitches, or unexpected changes in the project scope.

Attention to Detail: When it comes to video editing, attention to detail is essential. Editors should pay close attention to continuity, making sure that the audio and visual components flow together naturally. Small details can significantly impact the overall quality of the final product.

Emotional Intelligence: Understanding the emotional impact of scenes and sequences is essential. Video editors must be attuned to the nuances of storytelling, recognizing the emotional beats and ensuring that the audience's emotional journey aligns with the intended experience.

Chapter 3: Video Editing Process

Rahul Kumar (Studio Manager, Amity University Patna)

The method of editing in video production looks like a magical element, which helps enhance the quality of the video. This is footage in which your unedited video becomes an integrated and intriguing narrative. This chapter is very important. It tackles the pre-production planning phase with one another, ingesting and arranging the clip, and key editing methods. Before the shooting, you should plan a good editing process, which helps to make the video clear and attractive.

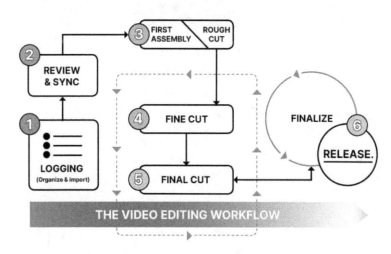

3.1 Pre-Production Planning:

Script and storyboard: Develop an extensive storyboard before the shoot. The storyboard helps to understand the situation very well before the shoot. A storyboard will help you visualize the final product and ensure you capture all the important shots.

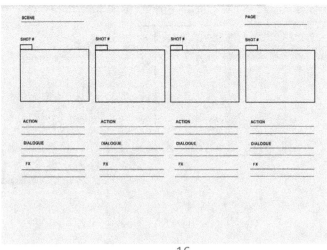

Shot list: Make a structure list with all the different shots you require, including each motion and perspective. This maintains the shot's accuracy and structure.

Location and Chronology: Before the shoot, it is important to finalize the location and timeline carefully to avoid any last-minute surprises.

Soaking in the arranging of footage after shooting is crucial to ensuring an easy editing process.

File Transfer: Transfer the video footage to your computer from the camera. To keep everything organized, pick a naming convention that is consistent.

Backup: Always create backups of your raw footage on an external hard drive or cloud storage to prevent data loss.

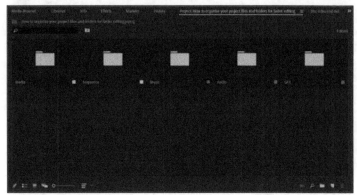

Organizing Footage:

Make Folders: Create a folder on your computer that makes sense for the project you are working on. For example, separate folders for raw footage, audio, graphics, and project files.

Label Clips: Assign your clips meaningful titles, add metadata like scenes, and take numbers. This will save you time when searching for specific shots.

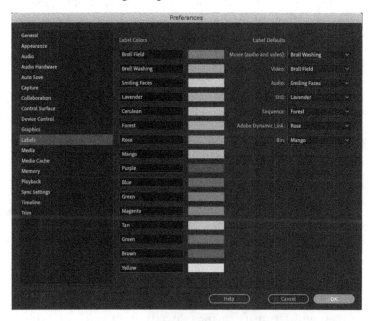

Bins and Sequences: In your editing software, create bins to organize your clips by scene, location, or type. Set up sequences for different parts of your project.

Project Panel Menu

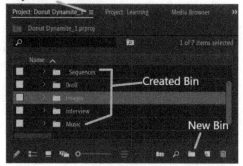

3.2 Ingesting and Organizing Footage

Ingesting and organizing footage is crucial for efficient editing. This step involves importing video files into Premiere Pro, sorting them into bins, and labeling them appropriately. Good organization at this stage saves time and effort during the editing process, making it easier to locate and work with specific clips.

This section will guide you through the process of importing footage into Premiere Pro, organizing it effectively, and setting up your project for success.

Importing Footage

The first step in ingesting footage is to import your video files into Premiere Pro. You can do this by:

Using the Media Browser: Navigate to the Media Browser panel, locate your footage, and drag it into your project bin.

Drag and Drop: Drag files directly from your file explorer into the Premiere Pro Project panel.

File > Import: Use the menu option to import files. This method allows you to import multiple files or entire folders at once.

Example: Imagine you have shot a documentary and have various clips stored on an external hard drive. Using the Media Browser, you navigate to the hard drive, select the clips, and import them into a new bin labeled "Documentary Footage".

Organizing Footage

Once the footage is imported, organization is key to maintaining an efficient workflow. Here are some strategies:

Creating Bins: Bins in Premiere Pro function like folders, helping you categorize and manage your clips. For example, create separate bins for interviews, B-roll, and sound effects.

Labeling and Metadata: Use labels and metadata to add information to your clips. You can rename clips, add descriptions, and use color labels to visually differentiate them.

Sequencing: Arrange your footage in the order it will appear in the final edit. This can involve creating rough sequences or assemblies to outline the structure of your project.

Example: For a wedding video project, you might create bins named "Ceremony," "Reception," "Interviews," and "B-roll." You can label all clips from the ceremony with a specific colour (e.g., blue) for quick identification.

Scenario: Editing a Music Video

Importing Footage: The director has provided multiple takes of the band performing their song, along with B-roll footage of the city. You import all these clips into Premiere Pro.

Organizing Footage: You create bins named "Performance," "City B-roll," and "Interviews." Within the "Performance" bin, you create sub-bins for each take. You label the best takes in green and the rest in red.

Setting Up the Project: You create a new sequence for the rough cut and drag your labeled clips onto the timeline. By organizing your footage ahead of time, you can quickly assemble a coherent rough cut, focusing on the best takes and visually interesting B-roll.

3.3 Basic Editing Techniques

With your footage organized, you're ready to start editing. Here are some basic techniques to get you started:

Cutting and trimming

Cutting: This is the easiest edit, in which extra portions of a video are removed to shorten or eliminate unneeded materials.

Trimming: To enhance your edit, adjust the start and end points of the clip to refine your edit. Maximum software allows you to trim directly on the timeline.

  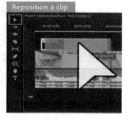

Transitions:

Transitions are an essential aspect of video editing, allowing you to seamlessly connect different clips and enhance the visual flow of your project. They can be used to convey changes in time, location, or mood, and add a professional touch to your videos. In this section, we will explore various types of transitions available in Adobe Premiere Pro, how to apply them, and some best practices for using them effectively.

Different types of transitions available in Adobe Premiere Pro:

Cut

Cross Dissolve

Dip to Black

Dip to White

Film Dissolve

Additive Dissolve

Non-Additive Dissolve

Wipe (including Linear Wipe, Clock Wipe, Radial Wipe)

Slide

Push

Fades and Dissolves: Use fades to black or white and dissolve transitions to create a smoother flow between scenes.

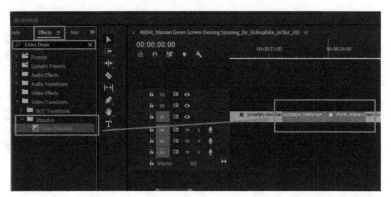

Wipe (including Linear Wipe, Clock Wipe, Radial Wipe): Wipes are more stylized transitions, like wipes, which can add a creative and unique touch, but use them sparingly to prevent attention.

Adding Audio:

Importing Audio: Incorporate your audio files, including sound effects, music, and dialogue. Keep them organized in separate tracks.

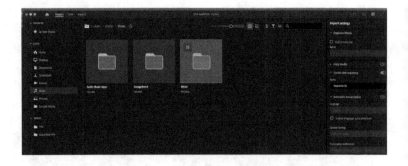

Audio Syncing: If you recorded sound by yourself or independently, then make sure your external audio or video footage is in sync.

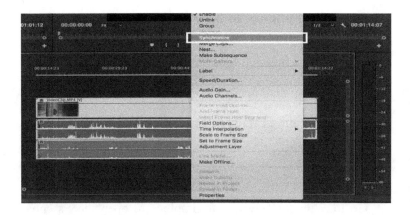

Basic Mixing: It is all about balancing dialogues with background music and sound effects and adjusting audio levels to ensure dialogue is clear.

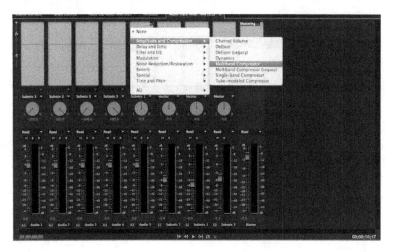

Titles and graphics:

Adding Texts: Use your editing software's text tools to add titles, captions, and credits.

Basic Illustrations: To boost your video and create basic graphics like logos, lower thirds, and animations

Here's a step-by-step guide:

Step 1: Open Your Project

Launch Adobe Premiere Pro.

Open your project or create a new one.

Step 2: Open the Essential Graphics Panel

Go to Window > Essential Graphics to open the Essential Graphics panel.

Step 3: Create a New Text Layer

Click on the New Layer button (a sheet of paper icon) at the bottom of the Essential Graphics panel.

Step 4: Add Your Text

A text box will appear in your Program Monitor.

Click inside the text box and type your desired text.

Step 5: Customize Your Text

Use the Edit tab in the Essential Graphics panel to customize your text.

You can change the font, size, color, and alignment.

Adjust the position by clicking and dragging the text box in the Program Monitor.

Step 6: Save Your Graphic

Once you are satisfied with your text, click OK or press Enter to finalize the changes.

Step 7: Add Animation (Optional)

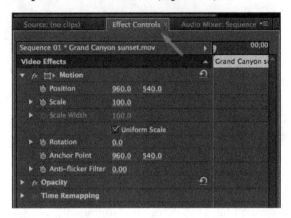

To add animation, select the text layer in your timeline.

Go to the Effect Controls panel.

Use the Position, Scale, Rotation, and other properties to create keyframes and animate your text.

Step 8: Export Your Video

When you're done editing, go to File > Export > Media.

Choose your desired export settings and click Export.

Graphics Example:

Use bold and contrasting fonts for visibility.

Add shadow or outline to text to make it stand out.

Use motion graphics templates (MOGRT) for dynamic titles.

Visual Guide:

Create New Text Layer

Add Your Text

Customize Your Text

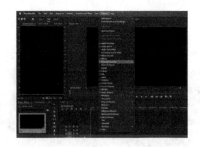

Conclusion:

If technical expertise and creative judgment are used in the editing process—planning in pre-production, organizing your footage effectively, and mastering basic editing techniques—you'll be well on your way to creating professional-quality videos. A continuous productive workflow is made possible from inception through conclusion by each step drawing on the previous one.

Chapter 4: Tools of the Trade

Rahul Kumar (Studio Manager, Amity University Patna)

To become a proficient video editor, you need the right tools. In this chapter, we'll explore the essential software and hardware that make up the toolkit of a modern video editor.

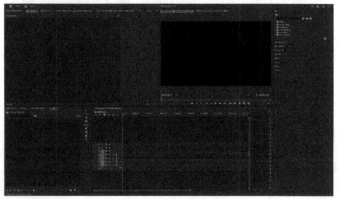

We'll also look at some of the most popular editing platforms available today.

4.1 Overview of Editing Software

Editing software is where the magic happens. This is where you cut, splice, add effects, and create your final video masterpiece. The right software can make your editing process smoother and more efficient. Here's a look at some of the key features to consider:

User Interface: A clean, intuitive interface makes it easier to navigate and find the tools you need.

Editing Tools: Look for software that offers a range of tools for cutting, trimming, and arranging clips.

Effects and Transitions: Quality software includes a library of effects and transitions to enhance your video.

Export Options: Ensure the software supports multiple formats and resolutions for exporting your final video.

Compatibility: Check if the software works with your operating system and hardware setup.

4.2 Hardware Components for Video Editing

While software is vital, your hardware setup plays a crucial role in how efficiently you can edit. Here are the main hardware components you'll need:

Computer: A powerful computer is essential. Look for one with a fast processor (CPU), plenty of RAM (at least 16GB), and a high-quality graphics card (GPU).

Storage: Video files are large, so you'll need ample storage. SSDs (Solid State Drives) are faster than traditional hard drives and improve your editing performance.

Monitor: A high-resolution monitor allows you to see your video in detail. Dual monitors can be beneficial for extending your workspace.

Keyboard and Mouse: Specialized editing keyboards and high-precision mice can enhance your workflow and speed up the editing process.

External Drives: For backup and additional storage, external drives are invaluable. Look for ones with fast read/write speeds.

4.3 Popular Editing Platforms

When it comes to video editing, the software you choose can significantly impact your workflow and the quality of your final product. Here's a look at some of the most popular editing platforms used by professionals and hobbyists alike.

Popular editing platforms

When it comes to video editing, the software you choose can have a significant impact on the standard of your final product and your production process.

Here's a look at some of the most popular editing platforms used by professionals and hobbyists alike.

Adobe Premiere Pro:

Adobe Premiere Pro is one of the most famous editing apps. It is mostly used by professionals in film and television. The industry loves it most for its versatile features and strong build quality.

Here are some of its key features:

Advanced Editing Tools: Premiere Pro provides a variety of options, like color correction, cutting, and audio editing.

Integration with Adobe Creative Suite: It seamlessly integrates with other Adobe products like After Effects, Photoshop, and Illustrator, allowing for a smooth workflow.

Customizable Interface: You can customize the workspace to suit your editing style, making the process more intuitive.

Getting Started Fast
Avid Media Composer
A Quick Introduction to Media Composer

Avid Media Composer: A foundation of the professional editing world, particularly in Hollywood, it refers to being known for handling large projects and complex workflows.

Some key features include:

Sturdy media management: Avid's massive organizational features make it a great choice for managing large volumes of media with its powerful organizational tools.

Collaborative Editing: It allows multiple editors to work on the same projects at once. It is a huge production.

High-precision editing: It has control over all editing operations, including color grading and cutting.

Offers detailed control over every aspect of the editing process, from trimming to color grading.

DaVinci Resolve:

Blackmagic Design's DaVinci Resolve has grown renowned for its powerful editing tools and robust color grading ability. It is an amazing choice for those who need both editing and post-production features in one package.

Some key features include:

Proficient color grading: This is known for the best color correction and grading tools.

Fusion VFX: By using this, you can produce amazing visual effects through the motion graphic tools.

Fairlight Audio: Integrated post-production solutions are supplied by powerful audio editing and mixing features.

Audio Editing: Add, adjust, and mix audio tracks, including music, voiceovers, and sound effects.

Titles and Text Overlays: Create custom titles and text overlays with various fonts, styles, and animations.

iMovie:

For newcomers or for those who are looking for simpler editing too, Imovie is a great option. For Mac users, it is free while offering easy-to-learn basic editing features.

Some key features include:

User-friendly Interface:

Its easy drag-and-drop feature makes it accessible to beginners.

Templates and Themes Pre-made templates and themes help you quickly create polished videos.

Integration with Apple Devices: Easily transfer projects between your iPhone, iPad, and Mac.

Photo and Video Integration: Easily import photos and videos from your iPhoto or Photos library for seamless integration into your projects.

iCloud Integration: Sync your projects across multiple Apple devices using iCloud, allowing you to edit on the go.

Social Media Sharing: Directly share your videos to popular social media platforms like YouTube, Facebook, and Vimeo.

Choosing the right video editing platform is crucial as it directly impacts the quality and efficiency of your editing process. Here's a deeper exploration of some key considerations:

Needs and Project Requirements: The choice of editing software should align with your specific needs and the requirements of your projects. For professional editors working on feature films, robust features like advanced color grading, multi-camera editing, and extensive plugin support (offered by tools like Adobe Premiere Pro, Avid Media Composer, and DaVinci Resolve) are essential. On the other hand, casual editors or beginners might find iMovie or simpler versions of software sufficient for basic editing tasks.

Skill Level: Different editing platforms cater to varying skill levels. Advanced software such as Adobe Premiere Pro and DaVinci Resolve offer extensive functionalities that require a learning curve. They provide professionals with tools for intricate editing, visual effects, and audio post-production. In contrast, iMovie and similar user-friendly platforms are designed for beginners, offering intuitive interfaces and simplified workflows to ease the learning process.

Financial Constraints: Budget considerations play a significant role in choosing editing software. Professional-grade tools like Adobe Premiere Pro and DaVinci Resolve typically require subscription fees or upfront purchases. However, they justify the cost with comprehensive features and frequent updates. Free or lower-cost options like iMovie and some versions of DaVinci Resolve provide accessible alternatives for those on a budget, albeit with fewer advanced features.

Unique Features and Capabilities: Each editing platform offers unique features that cater to specific editing needs. For example, Adobe Premiere Pro is known for its seamless integration with other Adobe Creative Cloud applications, extensive plugin support, and versatile timeline editing capabilities. Final Cut Pro is renowned for its optimized performance on Mac systems, intuitive magnetic timeline, and advanced color grading tools. DaVinci Resolve excels in professional color grading and has a powerful free version, making it popular among filmmakers.

In conclusion, the choice of a video editing platform should be a thoughtful decision based on your editing requirements, skill level, and financial considerations. By selecting the right software, you can effectively translate your creative vision into compelling visual stories, whether you're a professional editor or an aspiring content creator.

Chapter 5: Adobe Premiere Pro: Description and Tools

Rahul Kumar (Studio Manager, Amity University Patna)

Introduction:

Adobe Premiere Pro is a powerful and versatile video editing software widely used by professionals and hobbyists alike. Known for its robust features and flexibility, Premiere Pro is an industry-standard tool for creating everything from short clips to feature-length films. Let's dive into what makes Premiere Pro a top choice for video editors and explore some of its key tools.

Description

Adobe Premiere Pro is a non-linear video editing software that allows users to edit any part of their project in any order. This flexibility is perfect for complex projects that require multiple edits and adjustments. Premiere Pro is part of the Adobe Creative Cloud suite, which means it integrates seamlessly with other Adobe products like After Effects, Photoshop, and Illustrator. This integration is a significant advantage for editors who need to incorporate graphics, special effects, and other media into their videos.

Key features of Adobe Premiere Pro include:

Comprehensive Editing Tools: From basic cuts and trims to advanced color correction and audio editing, Premiere Pro offers a wide range of tools to enhance your video.

High-Quality Output: Supports various resolutions and formats, including 4K, 8K, and virtual reality.

Real-Time Editing: Efficient playback and rendering, allowing editors to see changes immediately.

Customizable Interface: Users can tailor the workspace to their specific needs, enhancing productivity and ease of use.

Key Tools in Adobe Premiere Pro

Premiere Pro is equipped with a plethora of tools that cater to different aspects of video editing. Here are some of the most essential ones:

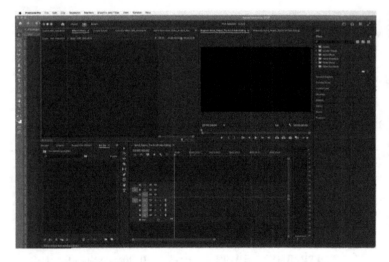

a. Timeline Panel

The Timeline Panel is where you assemble your clips and build your sequence. It's the heart of your editing workflow.

Tracks: Video and audio tracks where you place your clips. You can have multiple tracks to layer video and audio elements.

Sequence: The arrangement of clips and effects on the timeline that form your edited video.

b. Project Panel

The Project Panel is your organizational hub. It's where you import, manage, and organize your media assets.

Bins: Folders within the Project Panel to categorize and organize your clips, audio, graphics, and sequences.

Media Browser: A built-in file explorer that allows you to preview and import media files directly into your project.

c. Source Monitor

The Source Monitor is used to preview and trim your raw clips before adding them to the timeline.

In and Out Points: Set start and end points for your clips to determine which part of the clip will be used in the timeline.

Insert and Overwrite Edits: Options to add clips to the timeline either by pushing existing footage aside (insert) or replacing it (overwrite).

d. Program Monitor

The Program Monitor displays your timeline's output, showing you what your final video will look like.

Playback Controls: Play, pause, and scrub through your sequence to review edits.

Marking Tools: Add markers to highlight important points in your sequence for easy navigation.

e. Tools Panel

The Tools Panel provides quick access to various editing tools:

Selection Tool (V): Used for selecting and moving clips in the timeline.

Razor Tool (C): Cuts clips at the point where you click, allowing for precise edits.

Slip and Slide Tools (Y, U): Adjust the in and out points of a clip without changing its duration.

f. Effects Panel

The Effects Panel houses a variety of video and audio effects and transitions that you can apply to your clips.

Presets: Pre-built effects that can be applied to clips for quick enhancements.

Custom Effects: Create and save your own effects settings.

Lumetri Color Panel

The Lumetri Color Panel is a powerful tool for color correction and grading.

Basic Correction: Adjust exposure, contrast, highlights, shadows, whites, and blacks.

Creative: Apply creative looks and styles to your footage.

Color Wheels & Match: Fine-tune the color balance of your clips and match colors between different shots.

h. Audio Track Mixer

The Audio Track Mixer allows you to adjust the levels and effects for your audio tracks.

Volume Control: Adjust the volume levels of individual audio tracks.

Pan Control: Pan audio left or right.

Effects: Apply audio effects like reverb, delay, and equalization.

Timecode Snap Toggle Sync Lock

Panel Menu   Playhead

Video Tracks

Mute Track

Audio Tracks

Zoom In/Out Timeline

Source Monitor   Program Monitor

Project
Panel   Timeline

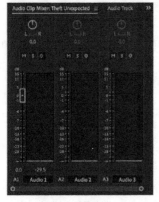

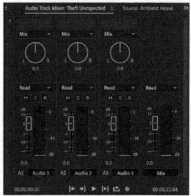

Audio Clip Mixer   Audio Track Mixer

Conclusion

Adobe Premiere Pro is a comprehensive tool that offers a wide range of features and capabilities for video editing. Its flexibility, combined with its powerful tools, makes it an excellent choice for editors of all levels. Whether you are creating a simple video for social media or a complex film project, Premiere Pro provides the tools you need to bring your vision to life.

5.1 Different Types of Transitions in Adobe Premiere Pro

Transitions are essential for creating smooth and visually appealing changes between scenes or shots in your video. Adobe Premiere Pro offers a variety of transition effects, each serving a different purpose and aesthetic.

Here's a look at some of the most used transitions:

Cut

Description: A cut is the most basic transition, where one clip immediately follows another with no visible effect.

How to Apply: Simply place two clips next to each other on the timeline.

Usage Example: Use cuts to maintain a fast-paced and dynamic feel in your video, such as in action sequences or dialogues.

Dissolve

Description: Dissolves create a gradual transition between clips, blending one clip into the next.

How to Apply:

Go to the Effects panel.

Search for "Dissolve" and choose "Cross Dissolve".

Drag the Cross Dissolve effect onto the cut point between two clips on the timeline.

Usage Example: Use dissolves to indicate a passage of time or to soften transitions in emotional or romantic scenes.

Fade In/Out

Description: Fades gradually transition from black (or another solid color) to the video (Fade In) or from the video to black (Fade Out).

How to Apply:

For Fade In: Place the "Dip to Black" effect at the beginning of the clip.

For Fade Out: Place the "Dip to Black" effect at the end of the clip.

Usage Example: Use fades to open or close scenes, providing a soft entry or exit.

Wipe

Description: Wipes transition between clips with a moving line or shape that reveals the incoming clip.

How to Apply:

Go to the Effects panel.

Search for "Wipe".

Drag the Wipe effect onto the cut point between two clips on the timeline.

Usage Example: Use wipes for stylistic transitions, often seen in classic films or to emphasize a change in location.

Slide

Description: Slides move one clip off-screen while the next clip slides in from the opposite direction.

How to Apply:

Go to the Effects panel.

Search for "Slide".

Drag the Slide effect onto the cut point between two clips on the timeline.

Usage Example: Use slides to add dynamic movement to transitions, useful in presentations or travel videos.

Zoom

Description: Zoom transitions magnify the outgoing clip while zooming into the incoming clip.

How to Apply:

Go to the Effects panel.

Search for "Zoom".

Drag the Zoom effect onto the cut point between two clips on the timeline.

Usage Example: Use zoom transitions for a dramatic effect, often seen in sports highlight reels or action montages.

Push

Description: Push transitions move one clip out of the frame while pushing the next clip into place.

How to Apply:

Go to the Effects panel.

Search for "Push".

Drag the Push effect onto the cut point between two clips on the timeline.

Usage Example: Use push transitions to maintain momentum and continuity, ideal for fast-paced videos like music videos or trailers.

Page Peel

Description: Page Peel transitions give the effect of turning a page, revealing the next clip underneath.

How to Apply:

Go to the Effects panel.

Search for "Page Peel".

Drag the Page Peel effect onto the cut point between two clips on the timeline.

Usage Example: Use page peel transitions for a playful or retro look, suitable for photo slideshows or whimsical projects.

5.2 Color Correction Techniques

Color Correction Techniques in Premiere Pro

Color correction is essential in video editing to ensure visual consistency, enhance mood, and convey storytelling elements effectively. Adobe Premiere Pro provides robust tools and techniques for achieving precise color adjustments, catering to both basic corrections and advanced grading.

Importance of Color Correction

Color correction plays a crucial role in video editing for several reasons:

Visual Consistency: It helps maintain uniformity in colors across different shots and scenes.

Mood Enhancement: Adjusting colors can evoke specific emotions or atmospheres, enhancing the narrative impact.

Correction of Imperfections: It corrects issues such as white balance, exposure, and color casts to improve overall video quality.

White Balance Adjustment: Correcting the white balance ensures accurate colors under different lighting conditions. For example, adjusting a scene shot indoors under artificial lighting to appear natural and balanced.

Color Grading: Applying creative color grading transforms the visual style of a video to match its thematic tone. For instance, adding a warm color tone to evoke a nostalgic feel in a flashback sequence.

Lumetri Color Effect: This powerful effect integrates various color correction tools into a single panel, including Basic Correction, Creative, Curves, Color Wheels, and more.

Color Wheels and Match: Adjust shadows, midtones, and highlights separately with precision. Use the Match feature to match colors between clips for consistency.

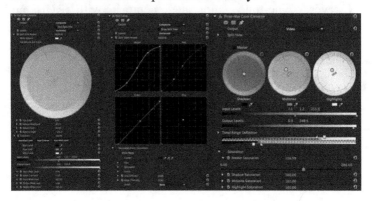

Color Correction Panel in Premiere Pro

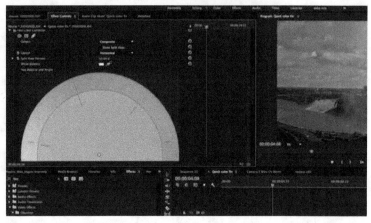

The Color Correction panel in Premiere Pro consolidates essential tools for precise adjustments:

Basic Correction: Adjust exposure, contrast, highlights, shadows, whites, and blacks.

Creative: Apply creative looks with built-in presets or custom adjustments.

Curves: Fine-tune color and contrast with RGB and individual color channel curves.

Color Wheels: Adjust color balance with separate controls for shadows, midtones, and highlights.

Step-by-Step Guide to Color Correction in Premiere Pro

Import Footage:

Start by importing your video footage into Adobe Premiere Pro.

Create a Sequence:

Create a new sequence that matches the settings of your footage.

Apply Lumetri Color Effect:

a. Go to the Color workspace by selecting it from the top bar or navigating to Window > Workspaces > Color.

b. Locate the Lumetri Color effect under the Effects panel (usually found in the Color Correction folder) and drag it onto your footage in the timeline.

Basic Correction:

In the Lumetri Color panel (usually located in the top-right corner), start with the Basic Correction section.

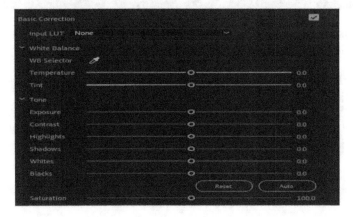

Adjust the Exposure slider to correct overall brightness.

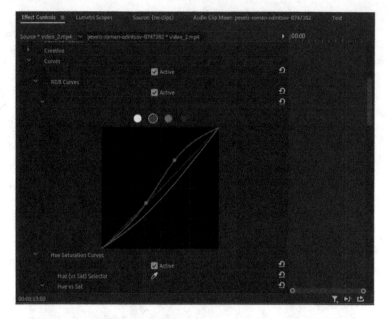

Use the Contrast slider to adjust the difference between light and dark areas.

Fine-tune the Highlights, Shadows, Whites, and Blacks sliders to adjust specific tonal ranges.

Correct the White Balance using the Temperature and Tint sliders to achieve natural colors.

Creative Correction (Optional):

Move to the Creative section of the Lumetri Color panel to apply creative looks.

Experiment with the Look Preset dropdown menu or adjust parameters like Fade, Sharpness, and Vibrance to stylize your footage.

Color Wheels and Match:

Navigate to the Color Wheels section to make precise color adjustments.

Adjust the Shadows, Midtones, and Highlights wheels individually to fine-tune the color balance.

Use the Match function to match the color between different clips for consistency (optional).

Curves (Optional):

Switch to the Curves section to further refine color and contrast.

Use the RGB Curves or individual Red, Green, and Blue curves to adjust specific color channels.

Finishing Touches:

Review your adjustments in real-time using the Program Monitor to ensure the desired effect.

Play back your footage to check for any adjustments needed for consistency and quality.

Export Your Footage:

Once satisfied with the color correction, export your video using Premiere Pro's Export settings to preserve the color corrections made.

Save Your Project:

Finally, save your Premiere Pro project to retain all adjustments and settings for future edits.

By following these steps, you can effectively perform color correction in Adobe Premiere Pro, enhancing the visual quality and ensuring your videos look polished and professional.

Mastering these tools in Premiere Pro empowers editors to achieve professional-grade color correction, ensuring videos not only look visually appealing but also effectively convey the intended mood and narrative.

5.3 Audio Editing and Mixing in Adobe Premiere Pro

In this subsection, we delve into the comprehensive audio editing and mixing capabilities offered by Adobe Premiere Pro. Effective audio management is crucial for producing professional-quality videos. This chapter covers essential tasks such as adjusting audio levels, applying audio effects and filters, using keyframes for precise audio adjustments, and integrating background music and sound effects seamlessly into video projects. Readers will gain practical insights and techniques to optimize audio quality and enhance the overall viewer experience.

Audio Types and Formats

In Adobe Premiere Pro, you can work with various audio types and formats, including:

Audio Types: Dialogue, music, sound effects, narration, ambient noise, etc.

Audio Formats: WAV, MP3, AIFF, AAC, and more. Premiere Pro supports a wide range of audio formats commonly used in video production.

Importance of Audio Editing in Premiere Pro

Audio editing in Premiere Pro is crucial for several reasons:

Enhanced Viewer Experience: Well-edited audio enhances the overall quality of a video, ensuring clear dialogue, balanced sound levels, and immersive soundscapes.

Narrative Clarity: Properly edited audio helps convey the intended message and emotions effectively, improving storytelling impact.

Professionalism: Quality audio editing reflects professionalism and attention to detail in video production, making videos more engaging and enjoyable to watch.

Difference Between Raw Audio and Edited Audio

Raw Audio: Unprocessed audio directly recorded from sources, containing imperfections like background noise, fluctuations in volume, or uneven levels.

Edited Audio: Processed audio after adjustments made in Premiere Pro, such as noise reduction, volume leveling, EQ adjustments, and adding effects. Edited audio is polished, coherent, and optimized for clarity and impact.

Step-by-Step Audio Editing in Premiere Pro

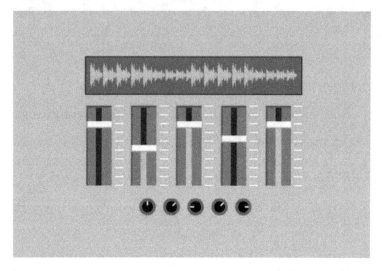

Import Audio: Import your audio files into Premiere Pro.

Create Sequence: Create a new sequence based on your audio specifications.

View Audio Track: Expand the audio track in the timeline to see waveform details.

Basic Editing:

Cutting: Use the razor tool (C) to cut unwanted sections or trim clips.

Moving Clips: Drag clips to rearrange or adjust timing.

Audio Effects:

EQ (Equalization): Enhance or modify audio frequencies using the Parametric EQ effect to improve clarity or remove unwanted frequencies.

Compression: Apply compression to balance audio levels, reducing dynamic range for smoother volume consistency.

Noise Reduction: Use the Noise Reduction effect to minimize background noise or hum.

Volume Adjustment:

Adjust volume levels using keyframes or the Essential Sound panel to maintain consistent audio levels throughout the video.

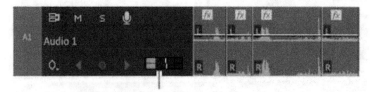

Track audio meter

Panning and Spatial Effects: Adjust panning to position audio in the stereo field or apply spatial effects for a more immersive sound experience.

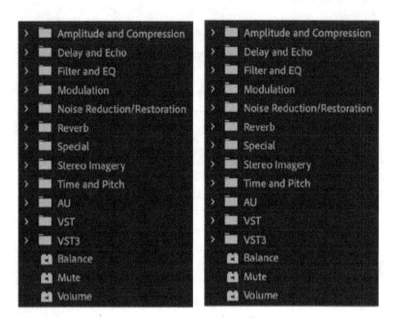

Audio Transitions:

Apply crossfades or audio transitions to smooth transitions between clips and avoid abrupt changes in sound.

Monitoring and Fine-Tuning:

Use the Audio Meters to monitor audio levels and ensure they stay within optimal ranges.

Play back your project to review and fine-tune adjustments for balanced, clear audio.

Exporting Audio:

Once satisfied with the edits, export your video with the edited audio using Premiere Pro's Export settings.

By following these steps, you can effectively edit and mix audio in Adobe Premiere Pro, ensuring high-quality sound that complements your video production and enhances viewer engagement.

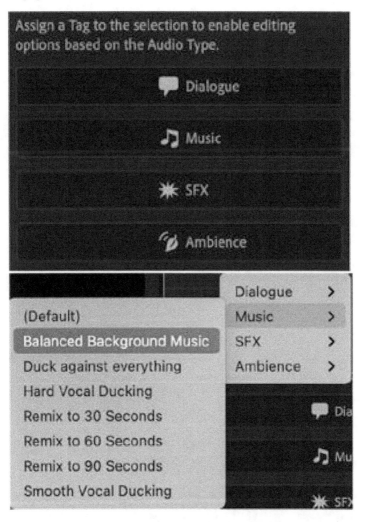

Chapter 6: Workflow Optimization

Rahul Kumar (Studio Manager, Amity University Patna)

Efficiency is key to successful video editing. In this chapter, we'll explore strategies for optimizing your workflow to save time and improve productivity. We'll cover tips for efficient editing, collaboration and project management, and troubleshooting common issues.

Tips for Efficient Editing: Efficient editing techniques can help streamline your workflow and maximize productivity.

Here are some tips to consider:

Keyboard Shortcuts: Learn and utilize keyboard shortcuts for commonly used commands and tools in your editing software to speed up your workflow.

Organization: Keep your project files, media assets, and timelines well-organized to easily locate and manage them.

Proxy Editing: Use proxy files for high-resolution footage to improve playback performance and editing speed, especially on slower computers.

Storyboarding: Plan your edits in advance by creating a storyboard or shot list to guide your editing process and ensure a cohesive narrative.

Batch Processing: Apply similar edits, effects, or corrections to multiple clips simultaneously using batch processing features.

Trimming Techniques: Use ripple, roll, and slip editing techniques to quickly trim and adjust clip durations without affecting the overall timeline.

Presets and Templates: Create and use presets, templates, and custom effects settings to save time on repetitive tasks and maintain consistency across projects.

Collaboration and Project Management: Collaboration and project management tools can help streamline communication, organization, and workflow coordination in team-based editing projects.

Consider the following:

Version Control: Use version control systems or project management software to track changes, revisions, and feedback throughout the editing process.

Cloud Storage: Store project files and media assets in cloud-based storage solutions for easy access, sharing, and collaboration with team members.

Collaborative Editing: Explore collaborative editing features in your editing software or use online platforms for real-time collaboration and remote teamwork.

Communication Channels: Establish clear communication channels and protocols for sharing updates, providing feedback, and resolving issues within your editing team.

Task Assignment: Assign specific tasks, roles, and responsibilities to team members to ensure efficient project execution and accountability.

Troubleshooting Common Issues: Encountering technical issues or errors during the editing process can disrupt workflow and productivity.

Here are some common issues and troubleshooting tips:

Playback Lag: Close unnecessary applications and background processes to free up system resources and improve playback performance.

Crashes and Freezes: Save your work frequently to prevent data loss in case of software crashes or freezes. Update your editing software and drivers regularly to fix known bugs and stability issues.

Media Offline Errors: Reconnect missing media files or relink offline clips to their original sources or proxy files. Double-check file paths and directory structures to ensure proper file organization.

Export Problems: Check export settings and file formats for compatibility with your intended playback platforms or devices. Render previews or use media encoders for smoother and faster exports.

By implementing these workflow optimization strategies, you can enhance your editing efficiency, streamline collaboration and project management, and effectively troubleshoot common issues, leading to smoother and more productive video editing experiences.

Chapter 7: Specialised Editing

Ribha Kumari (AIIMS, Patna) & Shasanak

Specialized editing techniques cater to specific genres or formats, enhancing storytelling and visual impact. This chapter explores different type of areas like Sports Editing, Documentary Editing, News Editing, Narrative Film Editing, Commercial Editing, WebSeries/Film Editing and Music Video Editing

Sports Editing

Sports is a word that contains a lot of entertainment but also emotions.

But have you ever noticed that when we watch any game on TV or smartphones, why do we get the feeling of climax?

You know that there is a team to make each climax scene, which we know as the editor's team. Sports editors try to make any sport look exciting through editing, and sometimes this attempt is successful.

There is no shortage of talents in our country; we can talk about any field. Well, there are few people who see their career as that of a sports editor.

So, let us understand and talk about some sports editing tips and techniques.

TIPS

1. Using different cameras

2. Capturing the image or video from different angles, shots, or movements

3. Music intensity

4. Use color correction.

5. Improve voice modulation for the commentator

6. Using graphics and overlays

7. Using transitions

Techniques

Capture the most important factors: The cameraperson focuses on the most important and exciting moments. of the game. They pay special attention to capturing the thrilling moments. Who became the highlight of the game?

Use several camera's angles: The cameraperson captures the moments from each and every side of the stadiums (indoors or outdoors). There are lots of angles, like low angle, high angle, eye angle, and many more. It helps to offer different points of view and improve the watching experience.

Utilize slow motion techniques: Slow-motion is one of the most important and best editing techniques, used mostly in sports like cricket, hockey, football, and many more. It can help highlight the brightness and emotion of key moments.

Maintain a quick pace: It means a quick clip was also added, which helps to create excitement.

Implement audio elements: For games like cricket, football, basketball, and more, consider adding crowd noise, commentary, and background music (BGM), which helps to enhance overall viewing.

Participate in graphics and overlays: In sports editing, one of the most important editing techniques is graphics and overlays, which refer to overall display statistics, player information, or

other relevant details.

Tell a chronicle: Pay close attention to the narrators, who convey the thrill and brightness of the game.

Scan This QR Code and You can watch Sports Interview Video Editing. You can see the Video and analyse how this video produce.

These are the few steps involved in sports editing:

1.Adding Footage

2.Arranging Clips

3. Analysing and Selecting Key/Thrill Moments

4. Cutting and trimming video

5.Adding Transitions

6. Adding Effects or Slow Motion

7. Tuning the Lighting and Color

8. Adding Audio Components

9. Including Graphics and Overlays

10. Improving Visual Effects

11. Sync Audio with Video

12. Exporting the Final Video

List of some software programs that are used in sports editing:

1. Sony Vegas Pro

2. DaVinci Resolve

3. Avid Media Composer

4. Final Cut Pro X

5. Adobe Premiere Pro

Documentary Editing

Documentary editing focuses on crafting compelling narratives using real-life footage.

Here's what you need to know:

Story Structure: Develop a clear story structure based on interviews, archival footage, and observational scenes.

Narrative Flow: Seamlessly integrate interviews, B-roll, and supporting visuals to maintain a cohesive narrative flow.

Authenticity: Preserve the authenticity of the subject matter while enhancing engagement through effective storytelling techniques.

Ethical Considerations: Respect the integrity and privacy of documentary subjects, adhering to ethical guidelines and standards.

News Editing

In today's generation, there are thousands of platforms where we can send messages to each other, understand them, and implement them. One of such platforms is the media platform, where we can express our views, showcase our talent, share some information, educate people, and entertain a large number of people.

Today, media has also been divided into many parts, like print media, digital media, and broadcast media.

But do you know how important the editing is to display any news in the media? So let us understand the importance of editing in news.

There are a few important guidelines to follow when editing news to ensure that your writing is informative, interesting and accurate:

Pay concentration on accuracy: Clarity is crucial when editing news stories. Verify all facts, sources, and information before publishing to maintain credibility.

Importance newsworthiness: Mark the most important news stories that will be important and timely for the audience.

Maintain a simple writing style: To make the news simple and easy for readers to understand. Try to write in clear and simple words.

Use attractive headlines: Always try to write an attractive headline, which helps grab the attention of readers quickly.

Include multimedia components: To improve the news and make it attractive, add some photographs, infographics, and other multimedia elements to enhance the visual appeal of your news content.

Examine spelling and grammar errors: Be sure to read carefully before publishing the news. To remove any spelling and grammar errors that can lower the quality of your work.

Some tv news graphics are as follows:

1. Tickers

2. Lower Thirds

3. Virtual Sets

4.overlays

5. OTS (over the shoulder) Templates

6. News Opens

7. Maps and Charts

8. Full-screen graphics

9. Full Screen Templates

10. Reopens

11. Bug (Channel Logo)

12. Mug

13. Weather Graphics

14. Promo and ID's

15. On Set Motion Graphics

16. Poll Results

17. Stock Market Tickers

18. Banners

19. Split Screens

20. Transitions Graphics

21. Countdown Timers

22. Social Media Feeds

23. Live Updates

24. Breaking News Alerts

25. Headlines

Here is a list of software programs that are used in news editing:

1. Sony Vegas Pro

2. DaVinci Resolve

3. Avid Media Composer

4. Final Cut Pro X

5. Adobe Premiere Pro

Narrative Film Editing

Narrative film editing plays a crucial role in shaping the story and emotional impact of a film.

Let's look at a renowned Indian film:

Example: Film: "Gangs of Wasseypur" directed by Anurag Kashyap.

Editor: Shweta Venkat Mathew

By studying the work of these esteemed editors and filmmakers, aspiring editors can gain insights into specialized editing techniques tailored to each genre.

Commercial Editing

Recognize your target audience: Before starting the editing process, it is necessary to know about your target audience.

Make sure your commercial targets a certain audience. And make sure the tone of the content and editing style suit the target audience.

Always make it inform: Commercial advertising has a limited amount of time to convey its message, so it's important to remove any superfluous imagery or speeches that would render the message potent and unambiguous.

Focus on narrative: Storytelling is essential in a short commercial. Create a good narrative that helps grab the public's attention.

Make full use of the outstanding image: In commercial editing, visuals play a crucial role. Make sure the footage is of good or high quality.

Use branding elements: Like logos, colors, graphics, phrases throughout the advertisement. This is good for greater brand awareness.

Introducing music and sound: Music and sound help to enhance the emotional impact and contribute to making it memorable viewing.

Examine and repeat: Once the commercial is edited, check it out among the target audience to gather feedback. Utilize this feedback to improve the advertisement.

If you want to build a career as a commercial editor, there are few tips that can help you succeed in this field.

1. Build a profile.

2. Build a network with professionals.

3. Learn technical skills.

4. Learn editing skills.

5. Always stay updated on industry trends.

Here is the list of some software, which are used in commercial editing:

HitFilm Pro

Corel Video Studio

Magix Movie Edit Pro

CyberLink PowerDirector

Final Cut Pro

Adobe Premiere Pro

Sony Vegas Pro

Avid Media Composer

Pinnacle Studio

DaVinci Resolve

Web-Series/Short Film Editing

Plan your editing process: Before you start editing, make sure and confirm you have a clear plan in place. Arrange footage, create a timeline, and add in a chronological way.

Maintain Consistency: To offer your viewer an enjoyable viewing experience with consistent style and tone.

Storytelling is essential: Pay close attention to the narratives of the web series and ensure that each and every episode is presented in a chronological way or not.

Create the best use of transitions: Transitions can help maintain the smoothness between scenes and viewers, maintain the flow of the web series rhythm, and keep viewers engaged.

Pay close attention to the audio: A better-quality audio is necessary for any type of web series for professional looks. Ensure that the background sound and music or dialogues are clear or balanced.

Experiment with multiple editing techniques: Use different types of unique editing techniques, like montage, split screens, and visual effects.

Feedback input: Represent the final edited episode among the audience and grab feedback to improve anything or the final product.

Music Video Editing

Coordinate the visuals with the music: Ensure that the tempo and beat of the music and the image are in sync. This helps create an engaging watching experience.

Use multiple camera angles: Use multiple camera angles for capturing the shots to create and maintain visual interest.

Use different transitions: Use multiple transitions, like cuts, fades, and wipes, for smoothness between shots.

Focus on lighting: Lighting helps to enhance the quality of video and create a good atmosphere and mood. Use artificial or natural light.

Location: A good location helps to make the video attractive; it all depends on the concept of the music.

Build networks and collaborate with artists: Collaborating with artists helps to understand the vision of the music.

Tell a good narrative: Write a good narrative according to the concept of the music.

Here is the list of some software, which are used in music editing:

1.   Adobe Audition

2. Audacity

3. GarageBand

4. Logic Pro X

5. Pro Tools

6. Ableton Live

7. FL Studio

CONCLUSION:

With the help of editing, we can make any raw footage for attention grabbing. Editing has its own contribution in every field, it has a different specialization. By using different editing tools and techniques, we can transform anything into a beautiful element. Overall, specialized editing refers to enhancing the quality of visuals and storytelling impacts.

Chapter 8: The Impact of Editing On Psychology

Shashank Parbat (Scholar, Amity University Patna)

"As you have read and thought about editing very well in the last few chapters and perhaps even understood it. But have you noticed how the effect of editing affects our behaviour, our expressions, and our psychological activities."

Like we spend a lot of time in making a video but after making the video, watching it may not be that much fun, if we do not try some editing on it."ohh sorry "you didn't care I am only talking about the video here but in that video if we add different types of angles, shot, music and colors effects then maybe that video will have a meaning, which will make people feel on their side. To attract, but it also depends on the content on which content you are making the video.

Well, let us know what impact editing has on our behaviour and psychological activities.

Our mind is always more influenced towards attraction, whether it is nature or human. Similarly, editing plays a big role in creating a beautiful scene in film/movies, which becomes the centre of attraction. And because of editing, our mind becomes very happy after seeing the beautiful delicacy inside a film.

"Well, let me tell you one thing, editing works like a fairy tale because it has to be used by itself, using it we can create as much surreal atmosphere as we want in a film. Not only in films, but by using it we can make any kind of poster or magazine cover page as per our wish"

Editing has a huge impact on our psychology. Somewhere an emotional attachment is formed, be it any emotion like sad, happy, fear, love, hate etc. But have you thought about how our mood changes when we watch movies? Some people will say it's because of hormones, but if we talk about the outside world, our mood also changes because of editing. When we watch a horror movie and someone appears in front of us, we get very scared.

But, did you notice that a horror-fear slow BGM (Background music) plays behind that shot and as soon as the shot comes in front, that BGM becomes louder, which impacts on our psychology due to which our behaviour changes and we get scared, for a few moments. Note: -The editing in a film is so powerful that it seems as if the moon is wrapped in love with the earth and can never be forgotten. Similarly, editing creates a relationship between the character and the audience.

So that the audience/viewers never forget, which increases psychological activities, and a strong connection is formed between the character/film and the audience.

Video editing is a great art, with the help of which we get to see and feel the cinematic experience. This is an art in which an attractive video is made by collecting raw footage and adding editing mixture to it. With the help of which people can be emotionally attracted and a memorable moment can be created.

8.1 Key Aspects of Psychology and Editing

Here is, some Key aspects which help to create an emotion and its impact on psychology.

Montage

There is a word in editing called Montage. Montage is a film technique that we use to convey emotional impact or to understand any complex ideas. There are many types of montages like, Intellectual, metric, rhythmic, tonal and overtone etc. All these montages have their own different meaning. All are used to make a meaningful video, which can create a canter of attraction.

Sound

The most important component of film editing is sound. Without it the entire film will be uninteresting and used for emotional impact which helps a lot in changing the mood and atmosphere of the viewers. Sound is such a unique component in any film, with the help of which we can connect people emotionally. Like in a movie, a person is crying without any sound, that too silently, and there is no sound in the scene, but no matter how much the person cried, it did not make much difference, but in the same scene, we added sad music/BGM. That scene will connect with us. This is the power of sound to make any raw thing to a point of attraction.

Transitions

Transitions are such an aspect within a film, with the help of which a meaningful sense can be created. Like creating a meaningful story by adding different shots. Also, we can add different types of transitions. Using transitions we can create a meaningful story. For example, in the morning scene we show sunrise and then sunset, hence the meaning is that from morning to evening.

Rhythm

In any film, a scene is very important and we record/click all those scenes from different angles, shot or then the movement. The breakdown of rhythm in any film is to give a break between emotions of viewers. Therefore, rhythm is always kept in a systematic way so that the narrative makes sense and an emotional connection is made between the viewers or creators.

Timing

Timing is also one of the most important components. At what time to add a sad song, or at what time to create what kind of mood or atmosphere. It all depends on timing and the concept of the story.

8.2 Color and Human Perception

How colors change Human Perception during watching movies/films/videos?

The significance of each Color is unique. White, for instance, is a combination of seven colors, VIBGYOR (Violet, Indigo, Blue, Green, Yellow, Orange and Red). There are several meanings associated with the colour white, including innocence, chastity, wisdom, and tranquillity. Mental, intellectual, and moral purity are on display here. While on the other hand, Black, which most people think of as the primary color. Wealth, respect, position, and authority are all symbolized by the color black. Concurrently, it might represent wrath, vengeance, or hostility. The color black is often associated with mourning and death.

Similarly, in video editing, all colors have different meanings. In some scenes white color represents peace and, in some scenes, it shows horror and ghosts. All colors have an impact on our emotions, we connect emotionally with all colors.

Chapter 9: Emerging Trends and Technologies

Mr. Soummay Ghosh (Assistant Professor, Amity University Patna)

Introduction of the Trends and Technologies
Earlier, the editing process was done on film labs and tapes that were on the big desks of analogue machines. Now more of a compact digital desk setup is introduced, and we have more power pushed on the CPU and GPU of the computer system. The only front end for video editing is now the video editing software, which is generally used with the help of a mouse and a keyboard. And with more technology developed, we use touch-screen features or touch pens or pencils. The most emerging trend in tech is the portability of a device. The size of the devices has been reduced to a very significant amount, and that is possible because of higher-processing chips of smaller sizes. From desktop to laptop to tablet, and now to a smartphone or mobile phone with all the high-speed wifi or 5G connection, you are ready to edit the videos. Applications like Adobe Premier Pro have also introduced the mobile version, Adobe Rush, for their users, and now they can edit videos on their smartphones themselves. There are multiple mobile editing softwares like KineMaster, Capcut, VN, and YouCut. Also, social media apps like Instagram and Facebook allow you to edit the reels in their apps before uploading the file. So the latest trends are the compact, powerful devices used for video editing. Also, in recent trends, we can see the rise and consumption of vertical videos. The industry-standard video editing software like Premiere, in their update, has also introduced a specific dedicated workspace for vertical video editing.

9.1 Introduction of AI in Video Editing

There are so many changes happening in the video editing industry. This revolution has just begun with the introduction of AI. AI as a tool in the daily lives of humans are like a extra helping hand. Applications and sites like Chat GPt by OpenAI started with text prompting to image and are now also going to render a new video from a text prompt. Let us first understand the basics: a video is made up of frames. So what is a Frame? It is the basic unit of a video, for example, 24 FPS (frames per second). This means that in 1 second we will have 24 photos. So what is a photo made up of? Now, one photo is made up of a basic unit called a pixel. So if the resolution of a picture is 4000*3000, this means that the camera is 12 megapixels, and vice versa. And these small units are digital when stored in a digital device or the computer itself. So the basic binary language of 0,1 is used to build the pixels from image to video, and so the AI using the LLM and its GPT is generating images and videos.

Now let us understand who is a video editor. The editor is the one who has a collection of assets and is provided with footages, then assembles it into a timeline to build the story using the methods of cut, copy, and paste. The simplest form of editing, removing the unwanted and adding the content in context. So remember that a video editor is not the one who is going to shoot a video for you. He is the one who has to compile the clips and edit them to showcase a final prodcut. So in case you lack a team member or are unable to get your friends to shoot a video for you so that you can show off your editing skills, Here comes the stock footage website that will help you out with uploading videos and images and let you practice with video editing. Examples of the websites are Pexel, Pixabay, ShutterStock, etc. Also, the AI tools will help you generate videos according to your story line, and then you can use the videos for editing purposes. As we grow in this fastest-growing world, we are often overloaded with work. So the AI tools come in handy in video editing as well. For example, if you are shooting a video in 1920*1080, that is in the ratio of 16:9 in landscape mode. Basically, for the YouTube video. Once your file is ready, you client, or if you are doing it for yourself, you yourself want it to be in 9:16 so that the vertical videos can be published in the Instagram reels and YouTube shorts. So now we have to make a new timeline sequence of 1080*1920 and copy all the footage to the new timeline. But now we have to adjust all the clips, and that is going to take a lot of time and effort, and the late update of Premiere helps you out. You can use the Auto reframe effect, and it will set the frame size while keeping the subject in the centre.

9.2 Latest Update to Premiere Pro

Let's talk about the latest updates to Premiere Pro and how the trends are making changes in the technologies.

1. **Addition of the Vertical Workspace in the Adobe Premiere Pro**

The addition of the Vertical Workspace in the Adobe Premiere Pro suggests that how much the influence of the new media and the vertical video.

We can access the workspace option from the Window menu and then select the vertical videos tab and then edit our video for social media.

A dedicated Option is available in the workspace icon on top right and we can see that the vertical option is on the second option from top. Which suggests how much priority this workspace is given. As the demand in the consumption of vertical video increases the supply of workspace for editing is fulfilled.

Just have a look on the option that is available in the workspace option

2.Addition of the Interactive Audio Fader in the Adobe Premiere Pro.

Earlier we have to use the keyframe to fade out the audio or use the default option of Default transition to apply fade out. But now with the interactive faders it's easy and faster.

3.Addition of the Emojis and Symbols in the Adobe Premiere Pro.

4.Addition of the Auto Reframe Effect in the Adobe Premiere Pro.

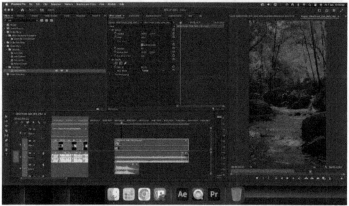

The Above is the option for Auto Reframe

The Auto Reframe option is Available in the effects panel, Under the video effect option under the Transform option.

For instance, if you are recording a 1920 x 1080 video in landscape mode, the aspect ratio is 16:9. For the YouTube video, essentially. When your file is ready, your client—or you, if you're working on it for yourself—desires it to be in 9:16 so that the vertical films can be featured in YouTube clips and Instagram reels. It is now necessary for us to create a new 1080*1920 timeline sequence and transfer all of the footage to it. However, we now need to edit every footage, which will take a lot of time and work. Fortunately, Premiere's late update will help.The Auto reframe effect can be applied to maintain the subject in the centre of the frame while adjusting the frame size.

List of Important Websites, Apps and Tools.

Here are the list of StockFootage websites:
Free Websites:

- Pexels
- Pixabay
- Coverr
- Videvo
- Dazed
- LifeofVids
- Unsplash (offers some stock video clips)

Subscription Websites:

- Storyblocks
- Shutterstock
- Adobe Stock
- Pond5
- Envato Elements

List of AI Video Tools Website:

AI Video Generators:

- Synthesia
- Colossyan
- Pictory
- HeyGen
- Runway
- D-ID
- Elai

AI Video Editing Tools:

- Descript
- Wondershare Filmora
- InVideo
- Peech
- Fliki
- Visla
- Opus Clip

List of Moblie Video Editing Apps:

- CapCut
- VN Video Editor
- InShot
- YouCut
- iMovie (iOS)
- LumaFusion
- KineMaster
- FilmoraGo
- Adobe Premiere Rush

Chapter10: Video Editing for Social Media

Rahul Kumar (Studio Manager, Amity University Patna)

Introduction: The Rise of Video Content

In recent years, video content has become the cornerstone of social media. Platforms like Instagram, TikTok, YouTube, and Facebook have all shifted towards prioritizing video in their algorithms, making it clear that video is the preferred medium for both users and brands. This shift is driven by several factors:

Engagement: Videos are more engaging than text or static images. They capture attention quickly and hold it longer, leading to higher engagement rates.

Reach: Social media algorithms often prioritize video content, helping it reach a broader audience organically.

Storytelling: Videos are powerful storytelling tools, allowing creators to convey messages, emotions, and narratives more effectively.

The   Impact   Of   Social   Media   Editing
The solution to this is quite straightforward: you don't want subpar work to be published. However, social media editing is more significant than merely a person's realistic desire to look   good.

It all boils down to content protection first. If valuable team time was used to create that piece of content, then equally as much effort should go into making sure it's as flawless as possible. This is true for both text and visual content, albeit it is more true for the latter. Similarly, a little misspelling or a misaligned typeface can give the impression that you are not careful to your followers. If your brand is perceived similarly, well, let's just say work won't be pleasant.

Secondly, there's the whole nebulous concept of "credibility" to consider. You want your content to reflect the same level of behind-the-scenes professionalism that goes into creating it.

10.1 The Power of Video Editing in Social Media

In the fast-paced digital world, where users are bombarded with an endless stream of content, capturing and maintaining audience attention is crucial. Video content has emerged as the most effective medium to achieve this. Compared to text or static images, videos are inherently more engaging, have a broader reach, and serve as powerful storytelling tools. This chapter will delve into the benefits of video editing for social media engagement, supported by real-world examples from the academic and music industries.

Engagement

Why Videos Engage Better:

Visual and Auditory Appeal: Videos combine visual and auditory elements, making them more stimulating than text or images alone.

Dynamic Content: Moving images and sound can convey a lot of information quickly, keeping viewers interested.

Emotional Connection: Videos can evoke emotions more effectively through tone of voice, background music, and visual storytelling.

Example: Academic Content

The Khan Academy is a prime example of how video content can transform academic learning. By creating engaging, easy-to-understand videos on various subjects, Khan Academy has revolutionized online education. Their videos often include:

Visual Aids: Illustrations, diagrams, and animations that help explain complex concepts.

Voiceover Narration: Clear and concise explanations that guide the viewer through the material.

Interactive Elements: Pauses for problem-solving and questions that encourage active learning.

These elements combine to create an engaging learning experience that holds the viewer's attention far better than a traditional textbook or static images.

Reach

Algorithm Preference:

Prioritization: Social media platforms like Facebook, Instagram, and TikTok prioritize video content in their algorithms, making it more likely to appear in users' feeds.

Sharing Potential: Videos are more likely to be shared than other types of content, further extending their reach.

Example: Music Industry

Billie Eilish's rise to fame can be partly attributed to her innovative use of video content on social media. By sharing short, engaging clips of her performances, behind-the-scenes footage, and music videos, she has managed to reach a massive audience. Key elements include:

High-Quality Production: Professional editing that highlights her unique style and personality.

Teasers and Snippets: Short clips that generate excitement and anticipation for full releases.

Focus on Key Messages: Editing allows you to cut out unnecessary parts and emphasize the most important aspects of your video. By highlighting key messages and removing distractions, you ensure that your audience focuses on what matters most.

Real-World Example: Instagram Stories

Consider a brand like Nike using Instagram Stories. A well-edited Instagram Story might include:

Text Overlays: Highlighting key messages or calls to action.

Subtitles: Making the content accessible to those watching without sound.

Transitions: Smooth transitions between clips to maintain flow and engagement.

Branding Elements: Consistent use of colors, logos, and fonts to reinforce brand identity.

By employing these editing techniques, Nike ensures that their message is clear and engaging, enhancing the overall user experience and driving better engagement with their content.

Building Curiosity

Curiosity is a powerful motivator that can significantly enhance the effectiveness of your social media posts. By strategically editing your videos, you can pique the curiosity of your audience, encouraging them to click on, watch, and engage with your content. Here's how video editing helps in building curiosity:

Teasing Content: Effective video editing can create teasers that hint at exciting content to come. By providing just enough information to spark interest but withholding the full story, you create an information gap that viewers are eager to fill by watching the entire video.

Unexpected Elements: Incorporating unexpected elements or twists in your videos can violate viewers' expectations and trigger curiosity. This can be achieved through creative transitions, surprising visuals, or unexpected narrative turns.

Engaging Thumbnails and Titles: The first thing viewers see are your video's thumbnail and title. Editing these elements to be intriguing and slightly mysterious can attract clicks. For example, using a thumbnail with a dramatic moment or a title that hints at a surprising revelation can draw viewers in.

Highlighting Key Points: Through editing, you can highlight key points or questions within the video that spark curiosity. For example, a text overlay that says, "You won't believe what happens next," can keep viewers engaged as they watch to find out the answer.

Real-World Example: Instagram Reels

Consider an Instagram Reel created by a travel influencer. Here's how editing can build curiosity:

Teasing Upcoming Locations: The Reel might start with a montage of breathtaking destinations, with text overlays saying, "Can you guess where we're going next?"

Unexpected Moments: Including clips that show unexpected or rare experiences, like stumbling upon a hidden beach or a surprise cultural festival.

Cliffhanger Ending: Ending the Reel with a dramatic sunset and a question, "What's around the corner? Stay tuned to find out!"

Intriguing Thumbnail: Choosing a thumbnail that shows a partially revealed landmark, making viewers curious about the full scene.

By using these techniques, the influencer not only captivates the audience's attention but also builds anticipation for future content, thereby increasing engagement and followers.

"Curiosity is triggered when people feel there is a gap between what they know and what they want to know. Professor of Economics and Psychology, George Loewenstein, is an expert in curiosity. He conducted a study into what triggers high levels of curiosity and discovered."

Professor of Economics and Psychology, George Loewenstein

10.3 Software and Mobile Applications for Social Media Video Editing

In the realm of social media, video content has become a powerful tool for engagement and storytelling. To create compelling videos, it's essential to have the right tools at your disposal. This chapter will explore various software and mobile applications that cater to different levels of video editing expertise, from beginners to professionals.

Desktop Software for Video Editing

Adobe Premiere Pro

Overview: Adobe Premiere Pro is a professional-grade video editing software used by filmmakers, YouTubers, and social media influencers.

Key Features:

Multi-Camera Editing: Seamlessly edit footage from multiple cameras.

Advanced Color Correction: Lumetri Color tools for precise color grading.

Audio Editing: Integrated audio tools to mix and balance sound.

Transitions and Effects: A wide range of effects and transitions to enhance your videos.

Example: Many professional YouTubers use Premiere Pro to create high-quality content with sophisticated effects and polished transitions.

Final Cut Pro

Overview: Apple's Final Cut Pro is a favorite among professional video editors, particularly those working on Mac.

Key Features:

Magnetic Timeline: Easy to organize and trim clips.

Motion Graphics: Integration with Motion for advanced graphics.

Comprehensive Guide to Video Editing and Career Development

Why do individuals choose to pursue a career as video editors?

The decision to pursue a career as a video editor is influenced by a combination of creative passion, technical aptitude, and the desire to contribute to the storytelling process. Individuals are drawn to video editing for several reasons:

Creative Expression: Reading the creation of visual storytelling, video editing enables people to expr ess their creativity. The ability to manipulate footage, control pacing, and create a compelling story provides a unique and artistic outlet.

Love for Storytelling: Telling narratives is an activity that many individuals have a natural attraction to. Video editing allows them to play a crucial role in crafting narratives, influencing emotions, and delivering messages through the visual medium.

Technical Proficiency: The technical aspects of video editing might appeal to people that possess an attraction with technology and an affinity to master editing software. The constantly evolving nature of editing tools provides opportunities for continuous learning and skill development.

Visual Aesthetics: Those with a keen eye for visual aesthetics find video editing to be a satisfying career choice. The ability to enhance the visual appeal of footage through colour correction, effects, and composition appeals to individuals with a strong appreciation for visual artistry.

Impact on Final Product: Video editors play a crucial role in the post-production phase, influencing the quality and impact of the final product. The sense of accomplishment that comes from seeing a project come together after hours of editing is a motivating factor.

Contribution to Various Industries: Video editing is a malleable ability that can be utilized by a number of businesses, such as internet content development, television, advertising, and filmmaking. This versatility allows individuals to explore diverse career opportunities.

Adaptability to Technological Advances: The people who desire to be on the forefront of industry trends will find interesting and dynamic surroundings through the swift advancement of editing technologies. Video editors often enjoy adapting to new tools and techniques.

Collaborative Nature of the Work: Video editing often involves collaboration with directors, producers, and other creative professionals. Individuals who thrive in a collaborative and team oriented environment may find satisfaction in the interpersonal aspects of the job.

Job Flexibility: Working arrangements could be versatile when applied to video editing. Freelance opportunities, remote work options, and project-based contracts provide individuals with a degree of autonomy in managing their professional lives.

Passion for Film and Media: A lot of people who decide to pursue a profession in video editing have a strong interest in movies, television, and visual narrative. The opportunity to contribute to the creation of impactful content aligns with their interests and fuels their career choice.

In order to put it bluntly, a video editor is a storyteller who utilizes expertise in technology, imagination, and teamwork to bring a visual narrative to life. Their role is to shape the raw material into a polished and impactful story that resonates with the audience.

Video editor looks like a mastermind head of the visuals. Which helps to enhance the quality of the videos. Video editor has a lot of potential, to turn any raw footage into a dazzling video. Video editor works in almost every field. Like education, entertainment, health, private companies, government companies NGOs, INGO's and for individuals also.

Top universities and colleges in India for studying Video Editing, Designing, And Journalism:

Amity School of Communication, Amity University Patna

Courses: Bachelor of Arts in Journalism and Mass Communication, Master of Arts in Journalism and Mass Communication

Amity School of Communication, Noida

Courses: Bachelor of Arts in Journalism and Mass Communication, Master of Arts in Journalism and Mass Communication

Indian Institute of Mass Communication (IIMC), New Delhi

Courses: Post Graduate Diploma in Journalism (English/Hindi)

Film and Television Institute of India (FTII), Pune

Courses: Post Graduate Diploma in Editing

Satyajit Ray Film and Television Institute (SRFTI), Kolkata

Courses: Post Graduate Programme in Editing

National Institute of Design (NID), Ahmedabad

Courses: Bachelor of Design (B.Des), Master of Design (M.Des)

Jamia Millia Islamia, New Delhi

Courses: Master of Arts in Mass Communication, Master of Arts in Convergent Journalism

Here are some highly recommended books on video editing that cater to various skill levels and aspects of the craft:

For Beginners:

"Non-Linear Editing- Cut, Crawl and Correction" by Badshah Alam & Sweta Priya

"Adobe Premiere Pro CC Classroom in a Book" by Maxim Jago

"The Technique of Film and Video Editing: History, Theory, and Practice" by Ken Dancyger

For Intermediate Editors:

"In the Blink of an Eye: A Perspective on Film Editing" by Walter Murch

"Making the Cut at Pixar: The Art of Editing Animation" by Bill Kinder and Bobbie O'Steen

For Advanced Editors:

"Art of the Cut: Conversations with Film and TV Editors" by Steve Hullfish

"The Lean Forward Moment: Create Compelling Stories for Film, TV, and the Web" by Norman Hollyn

Technical Focus:

"Avid Editing: A Guide for Beginning and Intermediate Users" by Sam Kauffmann

"Nonlinear Editing: Storytelling, Aesthetics, & Craft" by Bryce Button

Creative Focus:

Content Creation Strategies for Social Media by Soummay Ghosh

"Cutting Rhythms: Shaping the Film Edit" by Karen Pearlman

"Editing Techniques with Final Cut Pro" by Michael Wohl

These books cover a wide range of topics, from basic techniques to advanced creative processes, and should be helpful for anyone looking to improve their video editing skills.

Resource for this Book:

Book Refence:

In the Blink of an Eye by Walter Murch

"Adobe Premiere Pro CC Classroom in a Book" by Maxim Jago

Mass Communication in India by Keval J. Kumar

Content Creation Strategies for Social Media

Websites Reference:

www.open-innovation-projects.org

www.geekflare.com

www.Knowledge Workers - FasterCapital

www.universidadeuropea.com

www.geekflare.com

www.Macquarie University on 2024-05-10

www.open-innovation-projects.org

www.adobe.com/products/premiere

Thank You

Thank you for taking the time to read and engage with " The Art of Video Editing: Premiere Pro" Your interest and dedication to improving your video editing skills are truly appreciated. We hope this book has provided you with valuable insights and practical knowledge that will enhance your creative journey.

Feedback and Contact Information

We highly value your feedback and would love to hear about your experiences with this book. Whether you have suggestions, questions, or just want to share your thoughts, please feel free to reach out.

Contact the Author:

Rahul Kumar: contact2rahulkr@gmail.com

Your feedback is important to us as it helps us improve and continue providing quality content for aspiring video editors like you. Thank you once again for your time and support. We wish you all the best in your creative endeavors.

Sincerely,

Rahul Kumar (Author)
The Art of Video Editing: Adobe Premiere Pro

Stay Updated

Keep updated with the author for upcoming books related to Adobe Photoshop and the next edition of this book, which will focus on Adobe Premiere Pro and offer easy ways for video editing.